IS THERE
A PLACE
I CAN SCREAM?

IS THERE
A PLACE
I CAN SCREAM?

HAROLD MYRA

DOUBLEDAY & COMPANY, INC.

GARDEN CITY, NEW YORK

1975

Library of Congress Cataloging in Publication Data

Myra, Harold Lawrence, 1939–
    Is there a place I can scream?

    Poems.
    1. Christian poetry, American. I. Title.
PS3563.Y7I8   811'.5'4
ISBN 0-385-09988-6
Library of Congress Catalog Card Number 73-15477

CONTENTS

INTRODUCTION

Have you never felt like screaming? When you look at what's happened to you, perhaps? Or to someone you love who's had the enthusiasm for life crushed out?

Our screams seldom break past our lips. They burn in the belly; they sword-clang in the brain; they smolder in the chest.

"God is love."

How can he be? What loving God would set up a world with childhood cancer, bloody bayonets, empty lives?

We all sense—when we look with compassion—that something's incredibly, outrageously wrong.

Jesus himself one day screamed, "My Father, my Father, why hast thou forsaken me?" Modern man emits the same cry: Sartre and Camus, Pinter and Vonnegut—and we ourselves when we see clearly the ruined lives, the pains, the bitter wastes.

Out on a mountain, alone, there we could scream. Scream ourselves hoarse. Scream into the empty air. And finally stand with aching throat, futile, alone. But is there a place we can scream *and be heard?* Not just a place to let our cries escape like steam, but a place to confront, to find healing.

I walked one day in a woods and suddenly was confronting God with gut cries of *Why!* All the monstrous tragedies around me ripped out of my mouth. I demanded answers to why he'd made such a world. What was he trying to prove? Was this some silly game? Were we mice in a maze?

As I spoke out in utter honesty, at precisely that moment I felt Jesus' presence. The anger and questions boiling in me were what he had wanted to talk about all along. And, as we confronted each other, I found he had the same rage at injustice and crushed potential as I. In fact, it was his Spirit which made me so acutely aware they existed.

How foolish I had been to think God would somehow be jolted by my honesty, or insulted by my daring to question him to his face. He knows all the thoughts of my brain, even when they seem like heresy or rejection of him.

When one beats at God's door, demanding answers—when one tests Jesus on his promises—he finds truth and wholeness. Not, perhaps, the answers he had anticipated, but tantalizing truth, packaged in enigma and complexities. . . .

The prayers that follow are slices of my personal interactions with God. There *is* a place I can cry out. For answers. For wisdom. For his touch. There is a place in the Father's heart where screams not only pierce the air. They are heard by him.

IS THERE

A PLACE

I CAN SCREAM?

✠ HOW DO I TALK TO YOU? ✠

So here I am, Lord,
I'm ready.
I want to talk to you.
But how? What do I say,
standing here in this crazy carnival-world
of kewpie dolls and laughs,
bumper cars and whirlarounds,
with my ticket stamped in red—
no return: exit through horror show.

What do I say to you?
How do I say it?
Is it like talking to the President
—an awkward fumbling on the phone?
They say you're my friend—
just talk.
But I've never had a buddy I couldn't look in the eyes.
And, Lord, I've never talked to anyone who knows,
who *knows*
everything I'm thinking.
How do I talk to someone
who made the pancreas in my belly,

1

who keeps my frontal lobes from disintegrating?
Do I just say all those solemn things
I read on Easter cards?
Do I ask you for a better world?
A thousand requests for food for the starving?
An end to wars?
But you've been in charge for all these years;
who am I to butt in?

I heard about a young mother, Lord,
who got told in a hospital
that her little girl would die.
Her wonderful little girl—
who cuddled and ran and said silly things—
would die.
The doctor asked her how she felt.
She wanted to scream,
that's how she felt!
"Is there a place I can scream?"
"We have a chapel."
"I don't want a chapel!"
She didn't want to fold her hands,
to be quiet and "reverent."
She wanted to scream!
She wanted to scream at you, Lord,
to ask what in the world you were doing,
taking her little girl like that!

Lord, when I heard about her,
I wanted to scream, too.
You give little girls to love us,
then they get smashed in autos,
or germs eat out their insides.

2

What kind of a world did you dump us in?
What disasters they say *you're* behind.
Lord, if that mother can't scream
and ask . . .
If she's to sit in a chapel looking serene,
with acid-thoughts eating her brain,
why bother fingering a cross or a Bible?

How do I speak to you, Lord?
With screams and outrage?
Yes! Yes!
How else in an outrageous world?
Your Bible writers did.
They demanded answers,
Habakkuk and David,
Isaiah and Jeremiah.
They wanted to *know.*

My life is such a strange mixture, Lord—
like a child's play dough,
reds, yellows, greens, blues all smashed together,
screams and laughs and riddles and songs.
How do I speak to you from inside them, Lord?

I remember a girl's photo—
she looked eighteen,
all nose and cheekbone,
grimy in a print dress, fatigued,
but her face was brighter than a bride's—
such hilarious joy—
seeing her man emerge from a mine disaster!
Her exuberance joy-sobbed through her face,
and it reached into me like sweet honey.

3

How do I speak to you, Lord?
With yelps of laughter?
Yes! Yes!
I've sensed your joy,
like the joy on that girl's face,
and when you're flowing through me
with the freshness of being born again,
minute after minute,
new beginnings every day.

But sometimes you're so far away. . . .
I remember walking out of an exam once, Lord,
and standing there in the parking lot,
staring back at the big, brick building.
It looked just like I felt:
inert.
Cold stone.
Who gives a rip whether I passed or failed?
Whether I vomit or lust?

Should I talk to you then, Lord,
when I don't feel you around?
When all my emotions say life is
a gray mist to muddle through?

Then more than ever . . .
when you've withdrawn your presence,
to make me grit it out alone
with a naked will.
I can still speak to the God of living flesh;
I don't have to be a child
who lives by stomach and glands.

Lord, my days are a great jumble
of papers, hallways, soft touches and fears.

Want to hear about all that, Lord?
About the anger in my brain tonight?
The desire in my eyes this noon?
What will you tell me
when I share all I am?

This evening I walked
a patch of earth by a drainage ditch—
a rejected scrap of swamp—
but suddenly you had my eyes and throat and chest
all full of praise and wonder.

The late summer weeds, six feet tall,
had a thick, bright-yellow icing of sunflowers
spread all over them as if
a gleeful child with buckets of yellow frosting
had gone wild smearing the stuff—
all the way over to the oak trees
and up to the swamp water,
leaving cattails poking through like birthday candles.
I shoved my face into a sunflower—
a wild, untended smile button.
At my feet, a purple, ragged-edged blossom
looked like a bike wheel spinning,
with a crazy, unique center—
dozens of yellow eyeballs with red pupils,
like a science fiction monster.
A bug, small as an eyelash, crawled across the pupils;
a gray dragonfly helicoptered by,
landed on my arm, flew off.
I noticed green weeds—
kelly green, mint green, avocado green . . .
weeds and trees and pods buff brown,
kitten brown, heifer brown, cocoa brown, brackish brown.

5

Drops of water sparkled on petals.
I thought of movies made through microscopes
that showed the darting, feeding and shimmering life
of millions of creatures inside each drop.
Whole worlds were in my breath, blowing into the air.
Life! Colors! Smells! Crisp air!
The world was like gallons of ginger ale,
pressured from vigorous shaking,
fizzing with life,
buzzing with life,
exploding with life!

God, you are so full of life,
so full of creation,
you literally spill it out,
you fizz it all over me!
Millions of animals, bugs, germs, plants.
What a Creator you are!
How do I speak to you?
With praise?
With a clapping of hands?
Yes, Lord!
I'll cry and laugh and sing with you,
Father.
Heavenly Father.
You made my neurons, adrenalin, cortex.
You're ready to hear anything.
Lord, I'll cry and laugh and sing to you.

Thanks for making me.
Life is outrageous, Lord,
but it sure beats the alternative.

※ SOLOMON'S SONG ※

Somehow, Lord, when I was a kid,
they gave me the idea you were a prude;
a God embarrassed by sex.
But then I looked in the Bible.
You celebrate sex well, Lord,
in Solomon's Song.
It may be an analogy
of Christ's love for the church—
but it is also the song
of a lover's delight in his bride's naked body.
It's a song devoid of Victorian blush,
or even male chauvinism,
for the girl, too, describes her lover's body
with bold eroticism.

Your breasts are as two fawns;
you have ravished my heart, my bride.
Your lips drop honey,
honey and milk are under your tongue.
Your rounded thighs are a jeweled chain.
Your navel is as a rounded bowl
in which mingled wine is never lacking;

7

your belly as a heap of wheat,
Set about with lilies.
How beautiful you are, my love,
your breasts are as clusters of grapes.
I will climb into my palm tree,
I will take hold of the branches of it.
Your breasts shall be as clusters of vines,
the fragrance of your breath as of apples.
The roof of your mouth is like red wine.*

Lord, you celebrate the sensual,
and you made all things for us "richly to enjoy."
Yet Solomon the lover also says,
I adjure you
do not waken love until it please.

Lord, I sense the delicate wonders
when you smile on sex.
You watch two lovers on a beach;
the touch of fingertips says
"We like each other,"
and you smile.
You watch a kiss that's urgent, passionate
that says "We care deeply"
and your face comes alive with approval.
An embrace squeezes bodies tight from ankles to eyebrows,
and says, "We're sure of each other, forever . . ."
and you share the adventure.
When a bride and groom in clothes-gone passion
celebrate the marvelous bodies you created,
you look on delighted.

* From Song of Solomon, 4:5, 11; 7:1–9. The Modern Language Bible,
The Berkeley Edition. Zondervan Publishing House, 1969.

Lord, it's so marvelous—
sex with you smiling.
Lots more anticipation and mystery—
with a lover instead of a body;
a lifetime of purpose
instead of a romp in the hay.

※ JOHNNY ※

He came back to eighth grade that autumn
not boyish like us but thick-muscled.
We played horse and rider that first day back,
butting into each other, yanking, shoving,
but Johnny'd never go down.
He'd cleared land with an ax or some such thing,
and though he was still mediocre in sports,
no one shoved him too hard,
gentle Johnny.

I saw a horse once, Lord,
your remarkable creation
running with muscles
like living snakes trying to squirm out of his hide.
Years later, when Johnny came back to our town,
he was like that—
sinewed and hard; a man.
Johnny sort of happened to our high school,
entering with that broad grin and his Bible—
a huge one with leather-tooled cover—
and he'd do crazy things,
like letting *all* the girls board the bus before him.

11

He'd tell teachers why he carried his Bible,
and us, too, any time.

Lord, I don't know how much of that you told him to do,
but he cared. Wow, did he care!
An average student; a stereo nut,
he touched us like
a Fisherman Peter come to life.

I was best man at his wedding.
I remember sitting with him in the bedroom,
polishing shoes,
vowing protection against pranksters.
Johnny really cared about you, Lord,
there polishing his shoes,
exuberant about starting a new life
under your smile.
Was he making a mistake that day, Lord,
when we stood at the altar
and passed those rings around,
when we drank punch
and squirmed in tuxes and laughed?

They had a baby in about nine months,
and before the second one came,
I remember driving with him on a country road
as he told me he was a thousand dollars in debt
already.
They tried.
They seemed to try awfully hard, Lord,
going to New Jersey for a better job,
always trying some new solution.
But every time I'd hear about them,
they were fighting.

I'd see him in church once in a while,
but we only shook hands
and talked about his job and babies.

Maybe they never had a chance—
teen-agers getting married.
What did they know, Lord,
about how fast you can be a thousand dollars in debt?
How fast babies start pressures?
How could they know their frustrations were normal,
not each other's fault?
Johnny never had a chance.

Or did he?
Did he ignore you a thousand times?
Remember the last time I was with him, Lord,
that cold winter day?
We sat talking in his old car, parked in a coal yard.
I couldn't see his face or eyes,
but I knew the old Johnny
had been slowly strangled somehow.
"Come with me to Chicago," I offered.
But I didn't press him.

Some say he did it on purpose—
let the gas kill him in that cabin he was building.
But I doubt it.
A few days before he died
my mom watched him in church,
sitting there with his little daughters beside him,
smiling, singing hymns.

Why'd you let Johnny die, Lord?
Why the rift between lovers?

The crushing of children?
Why'd you let Johnny make such mistakes?
He loved you.
I thought you loved him,
Were supposed to keep him and all that,
all through life.
The hymns we sang together said that.

But I'll admit Johnny was weak.
We talked once, walking through autumn goldenrod,
about his drifting from you,
and I was laying it on him—
how miserable he would always be,
fighting you.
And Johnny wept,
and opened himself to you.
But did he fight you, Lord?
Was he making choices all along
that he knew were wrong?
But, Lord, aren't we all weak like that?
Johnny was just that kind of guy—unsteady.
Maybe that kind of guy gets that kind of pain.

And I get mine in the head.

Enigma. Mystery. Frost patterns on colored windows
that tell no story . . .
not yet.
What are you doing in our lives, Lord?
Anything?

GROUCH

The early morning Grouch–
it's bitten both of us, Lord.
Now, Jeanette tries to kid me a little
as she gets out of the car:
"Don't stay mad at me all day. Ok?
I'll only be mad at you for a minute."

My throat rumbles, "I won't."

"Promise?" she asks,
trying to break through.
"It's not good for you to stay mad."

I love her, Lord.
But today I'm a grump.
Then act loving whether you feel like it or not.
Is that what you're telling me, Lord?
But how do I keep the grump out of my voice?
You know I tried to sound half humorous
when I said, "Oh, don't give me that!"
But it sounded almost nasty.

If you really want to change,
admit your weakness to her.
Ask for help from her.
Yes, from HER!

Lord, I guess it's easier to talk to *you*
than to show a loving attitude.
What's in me, Lord, that makes it so hard
to say I'm wrong?
It seems silly.
I'd rather sulk like a little boy.

Lord, I know you want us,
when we grate on each other,
to confront,
to openly say what's creating anger.
Help us to show love
right in the middle of all that brutal honesty.

Teach me, Lord,
about loving acts,
and loving words.
It's easy to be a lover
when you're in the mood.
Help me, Lord,
to love the girl I love
on mornings like this. . . .

※ ARE YOU OUT THERE? ※

Sometimes, Lord, I feel all alone,
as if all there is in the universe
is me . . .
and maybe, *just maybe,* you.
I feel as if I'd just awakened
in a room-sized box floating like debris in space—
just me, the box, and blackness . . .
drifting who knows where or how.
But right outside the wall,
in the eerie, unnerving darkness,
I hear breathing.
Ominous sounds.
And I chew my fist.
The walls could implode on me any second.
Or you could breathe on them,
and the whole room would shrivel.
Is that you out there?
What are you doing?
What would you be like
if I put my fist through this wall
and met you?

These walls—how silly they are,
these membranes between me and death.
They're wet wads of tissue,
purples, reds, greens, browns, golds,
all running together like at Woolworth's,
but with people, dogs and mushrooms,
stereos, turtles, babies mouthing, grinning, being,
but none are me,
none are listening inside my soul
to that nerve-rasping breathing out there.
Is it you?

I hear you out there,
moving around, laughing sometimes.
Am I mad?
Am I really all alone here,
and everything that exists is just here
to tempt my brain with insoluble riddles?
This box, so fragile.
Don't breathe on it!
Don't yank me to you,
naked, just me,
Awesome Maker of universes,
at whose glance mountains melt, quasars splutter.
Who are you out there?
A terrible lion ready to shred me,
to rip my flesh, snap my bones,
your holy carnivore breath deadly
to a man of unclean lips?

God, who are you?
Are the songs right—
are you up there sweeping out my mansion?
Will you be a gentle hotel clerk

showing off the rooms?
Or maybe like Grandpa Time in flowing robes,
hoping I enjoy the view?

Are you like a parent who says,
"It's ok. Relax"?
Or are you like a hanging judge?
Will meeting you be pure joy—
home at last?
Are you a hilarious prankster
who will clap your hands and throw me in the air
like a laughing baby,
and say, "It's ok. It's ok.
What were you worried about?"

Will you be a holy, terrible God,
spreading joy mixed with awe and fear?
Are you an aggrieved lover,
with anger scalding hot,
righteous, indignant?

Watergate. I think about each man, Lord,
being questioned under lights,
lights, lights, lights, lights, lights, lights,
showing every hair on his sweaty face,
every tremor of his sick smile.
How'd he know they'd be probing every memo,
every comment?
Every little angle of his life
spread out like a smorgasbord for millions.
The questioners staring like pinch-eyed judges,
watching him squirm, evade, plead inside himself,
Why was I such a fool?

19

Is that how it's going to be, Lord,
in front of you?
Judgment day.
Crowds.
But no cross-examination necessary,
cause they've got color videotapes?
Is that how it will be—
billions of creatures watching
as I choose myself,
always my own self,
in a thousand scenarios when you were there,
needing bread, or water, or love?
Are you really a consuming fire, Lord,
your hot anger burning through my hollow being?
Will your awful purity
be more terrifying than Satan's racks?
Terrifying to the core of my selfishness?
Jesus, you talked an awful lot about doomsday,
sheep and goats,
broad way and narrow,
your rewarding and punishing.
Is your face so dark and angry?
Or will it light up
with smiles and recognition?
Will you have a face?

Are you there, Lord?
Sometimes I wonder.

But I hear you breathing again.
I know you're out there.
And Hitler as well as Jesus did live,
and if life has no moral thrust,
there is nothing, nothing, nothing.

And if nothing,
why not shoot cyanide into our veins,
burst through to rest?

I wouldn't burst into rest,
I know it.
I'd smash right up against you.

I search in your book, Lord,
and I find some men who met you face to face.
And you are no grandfather cuddling us.
You are no kindly gent sweeping out rooms.
They found you in awesome smoke and fire:

Ezekial saw you all glowing bronze
and fell on his face before you.
"Stand up," you told him.

Isaiah saw you
in smoke and glory of strange creatures,
and he cried out,
"I am a foul-mouthed sinner!"
but you touched his lips with hot coals
and said,
"Be clean."

Daniel saw blinding flashes from your eyes,
like lightning,
and your voice like a vast crowd roaring,
and he felt terror.
But you touched him,
lifted him trembling to his hands and knees,
and you said,
"Stand up. Don't be afraid."

21

John saw you with eyes penetrating like fire,
your face like the sun,
and he fell at your feet like a dead man.
But you laid your hand on him and said,
"Don't be afraid."

Lord, will you reach out to me?
Will you touch and lift me,
and say, "I love you,
don't be afraid"?
Will you touch my lips and eyes?
And will I say with David,
"I shall be satisfied,
when I awake with thy likeness"?

Any second it could happen.
Everything gone.
Pencils. Shoes. Shirt. Radio. Friends.
Gone.
Nothing but you.
And me.

Lord, reach out. Touch me.

※ SUPER FLEA ※

Lord, I understand you've made fleas
that if man-size
could leap buildings in a single bound.
And they can hop for days at a time,
600 times an hour,
and never get tired.
All it takes is a propulsion system
like a rubber band being cocked,
then let go—
ZOWEE!
and off he flies,
with up to 140 G's on him!

One little flea, Lord.
A pesky mite to stamp on,
or scratch at,
or scream at, maybe.
To tell you the truth,
I don't know why you made such parasites anyway.
But that little flea says,
as powerfully as DNA,
or a brain,

23

or a drop of sperm,
that all this is more than accident.

Lord, when I look at the vastness of your worlds,
I get tempted to think it's all random,
all just happenings,
and you're just a dream.
But how'd that flea get his super propulsion?
And did the eye *evolve*
without any help from you?
That staggers my mind.
You *had* to be in there somewhere!

The wonders of your world, Lord.
What a continuous marvel.
What a creative Creator you are!

SURPRISE!

A snack–maybe a Coke, or last night's meatballs.
But I'm still full of chocolate pudding.
TV. Maybe the Cousteau special.
Or I could straighten my desk,
talk with Jeanette,
drive to the store,
write to Dave.

Lots to do–
but who cares? The zest is gone.
Lord, when I'm ignoring you,
I'm a dead fish floating.

I once watched a boy see his first kitten.
He stared and moved toward it,
then looked up at me and laughed,
a huge, delighted grin of a laugh.
What a thing to discover–
this multicolored package of lively fur.

I watched a little girl meet her first gorilla.
She was awestruck.

She opened her arms as wide as possible,
declaring,
"He's bigger than the whole world!"

Lord, I love it
when you smash through my boredom.
Your surprises are hidden to those who ignore you,
but they're as real as kitten's fur—
and awesome as gorilla's teeth.

Lord, sometimes you crash into my life
with lumberjack boots.
Sometimes you tiptoe in,
and if I don't listen carefully,
I miss you.
Enliven this dead fish, Lord.
Let me swim with your life.

❊ BEASTS AND BEAUTIES ❊

Lord, I never said anything nasty,
but I admit I never accepted her—
not as an equal.
She was a spinster at seventeen,
and she always would be.
She reminded me of a skinny, leafless tree
trying to grow on an expressway divider—
surrounded by concrete and grumbling cars,
roots into grass so sparse and exhaust choked,
other life avoided her.
Even as a little kid,
she must have been like that,
alone, avoided,
life roaring past her with no apology for the fumes.
Who hugged the girl but her mother?
Her face was angular, all bones, dark shadows,
touches of black facial hair.
In a carful of kids,
I ducked to the back seat
to make sure no one got the idea
she was with me.

She became very religious
and even went off to Bible school.
I remember driving her somewhere
while she was full of joy and resolutions.
"No Bible, no breakfast," she told me,
saying how vital you were to her.
And that summer she got pregnant.
That was the end of her bright new life—
you don't go off to Bible school
with a baby in your tummy.
I wondered, then, unkindly,
what hard-up misfit had touched her,
had treated her like a person,
had held her with affection,
and suddenly nothing mattered to her
as much as being
held. . . .

I don't know about that summer.
But one thing she needed
besides her Bible and prayers:
Christ come alive in friends.
Could I have touched her on the shoulder,
laughed with her?
Could the girls have been more like sisters
than Mothers Superior?
Maybe she could have found a love
that wouldn't have left her pregnant and alone.
Maybe she could have been strong,
and chosen for herself,
if she'd found more of you in some of us.

Beautiful kids have more fun, don't they?
They're the only ones who drink Pepsi,

laughing like Nordic gods.
They're the only ones who splash down rapids
with glistening teeth to commercial music.
They're the only ones who tan so sexily.
You tell us, Lord,
"Don't be conformed to the world's standards;
don't be pressed into its mold,"
but it's been flashed into our brains
in such volume the images drip over the edges.
And the grubby look of jeans
can't change the mental machinery
and the vicious social games we play.

Yesterday,
I sat in a restaurant full of college kids
and a group of girls noisily sat down.
They looked over at a pimple-faced boy two tables away,
and I heard one snicker,
"Oh, yuck!"

How many times does a boy have to hear *Oh, yuck!*
before he believes—really believes—
"I am garbage.
I am a walking, living, breathing pile of trash."

A couple weeks ago, in this same restaurant,
three boys and two girls came in.
One girl, fairly attractive, slid into a booth,
and a boy slid in with her.
The other girl slipped in opposite them,
but neither boy would slide in by her.
They looked at each other awkwardly.
Neither wanted to sit by her.
In a few seconds, one boy succumbed,

but everybody knew it wasn't by choice;
his reputation was safe.

I wonder, Lord,
what those seconds did to that girl.
Did she feel like shrinking into her purse?
Did those hesitations
move her toward hating herself?
Lord, why do you let a girl's beliefs about herself
be found in her mirror?
One girl believes herself a princess,
and holds court.
Another girl believes,
because of the shape of her nose,
the roughness of her cheek,
that she's a dog.
And it permeates everything in her life
this self disrespect.
Lord, how could you put all those glands in her,
those longings to be held,
and have her clasp empty air all her life?

I read a survey once that half the girls in America
never land one date in high school.
Yet our culture screams
"A boy must touch you, kiss you,
or you're not really alive."
You hear the cruel asides in locker rooms,
"So many dogs around this school."

A girl rode our bus in high school.
She had orange, fuzzy hair,
wore outlandish clothes from her mother,
and she drenched herself in perfume.

I suppose she was saying,
"Look at me! Look at me!
I'm not only human, I'm a woman!"
One day, she exploded at a senior boy.
She couldn't articulate cleverly—
it all came out in clichés like,
"You, Mr. High and Mighty,
you think you're everything!"
Later I asked her brother,
"Have I ever given you that feeling—
that I'm better than you?"
He never did answer me,
but looked out the window at the trees.

I met this fuzzy-haired creature once,
alone between classes,
and asked her where a certain teacher was.
With just the two of us talking,
suddenly we were two humans,
like birds on the same rock,
no audience to play to,
no worries of who would be associated with whom.
She answered my question,
and we talked a minute.
Although our words were no different,
the chemistry was altered.
For that moment. For about ninety seconds.
But never again.

How much have I grown, Lord,
beyond seeing friendships as plus or minus status coupons?
Surely I don't still act that way!
But do I find more sophisticated ways
to shun the misfit?

Do I love the nobody,
the social embarrassment?

Lord, help me not to be molded
by the world's ad campaign of lucious lovelies
and wind-blown men on boats and horses.
By your Spirit, help me to see
beneath skin and posture, style and hair.
For I'm told you yourself, Jesus,
were nothing for looks.*

* Isaiah 53:2

✇ LOVIN' YOUR MUSIC ✇

Beside me at a stop light
a boy in a Mustang tapped his steering wheel,
his head bouncing vigorously.
It looked eerie.
Our windows were closed—
I was sealed from the music in his car,
so his pantomime looked crazed,
surreal in the traffic.

Today I sit in the library.
Kids stare at notebooks.
Librarians put cards in machines.
In the park across the street,
new flowers dance
and the spring air invites escape.
But everyone is self-possessed, businesslike—
trapped by deadlines and duties.
Except for the boy with the earphones!
He's sitting at the record counter
undulating happily.
Rhythm rocks through him

as he unabashedly enjoys,
and stares at us worker ants.

In the traffic of the city, Lord,
and in the people traffic every day,
do I listen to your music?
Or do I care so much what people think
that I'm afraid of looking weird?

Lord, am I so wrapped up in your music
that I feel the *joy* you promised,
even in the fumes and doldrums—
even in maddening frustrations?

Help me, Lord, to listen,
to tap my fingers,
to bounce a little.
And not to worry what people think.

✖ WHY THE JET-SEX ENGINE? ✖

Thanks, Lord,
thanks for our sexuality
for the whole marvelous idea of our male/femaleness.

You've made something beautiful, Lord.
But I wonder—
why'd you make it so massive,
my need to touch a woman,
to look at her naked flesh,
to fondle and merge?
I look around at my friends,
eating, reading, jabbering,
and I know and they know that within us,
the force dances into our brains,
inanely, merrily leading thoughts
to a thousand variations of sex adventures.
All the studies say
we're constantly thinking of it—
and sales of skin books
show our omniverous hunger.

Why make sex so powerful, Lord,
like a twenty-pound gland in a hundred-pound body?

Did you mis-engineer, Lord?
Or are we misdirected gluttons?

Lord, your ways are best.
I fully believe it.
Yet there's still the pressure.
There's still the wanting it all the time
—at the oddest times
and the most inconvenient places . . .
wanting it all through life.
Why this 727 jet-sex engine
in my Volkswagen body?
Why must it keep grabbing my brain?
It's gotta be powerful, sure
to keep the species going.
But if you'd toned it down a little, Lord,
I'm sure I'd still get around to my part.

I guess I know at least one answer.
All my spiritual longings
draw me to joys in you—
deeper, more powerful than anything on earth.
My yearnings for you conflict with my bio-body,
that seeks coupling and food,
and can be enslaved by them.
You died to make us gods,
with resurrection life
pulsing in bodies, in brains.
And you call me to walk among temptations—
to control the forces
instead of becoming enslaved to them.
To eat,
but not become a glutton.
To love,

but not become obsessed.
To achieve,
but to love others more than myself.
Paradox!
Your world is full of it—
tension and conflict, drive against drive.
And sex is full of paradox:
"Get yours, but don't use each other."
"Live with your drives, but care more about her."
What you demand of me, Lord,
is a soldier's alertness in treading a minefield.
It's only possible close to you,
for only you know where the death traps are . . .
and where the deepest love is.

※ BUGS ※

I sit in park grass,
my back against a tree,
feet propped on a huge cement turtle.
A bug crawls on my knee,
long, skinny, black,
with bent legs, wire-like feelers.
A squat, light-green bug on my arm,
very small, segmented,
with baby fuzz on his head,
flutters his wings to fly off,
then decides to explore the forest of my hair.

Bugs.
If I were to sit here on the grass and say,
"Ah, today I will create some bugs,"
I suppose I'd start with a round one.
I'd put some legs and feelers on it,
add a color.
Then maybe I'd make an oblong one.
Then a thin one, like a strip of spaghetti.
Then a curvy one, like a fingernail clipping.
I'd spread primary colors on them,

and a few tints and hues,
combinations of reds, yellows, blues.
Then what?
I'd run out of ideas fast.
I'd soon have to borrow ideas from you.
But Lord, when do *you* run out of creativity?

As soon as I look into the grass,
I see a crazy, Picassoesque variety.
Beetles, lady bugs, ants,
wispy, airy things that float,
and wriggly, wormlike squirmers.
What imagination you have!
Bugs exactly like twigs.
Prehistoric, armor-plated miniature dinosaurs.
Colors, combinations of shapes and sizes
to outdo Renoir, Disney and Peter Max.

Just bugs.
And then there are birds and fish and . . .

❈ FUMBLING QUARTERBACK ❈

Sometimes, Lord, I feel like a quarterback
with the ball glued in my hands,
never seeing open space,
just getting chased all the time by the Bruisers,
always scrambling but never getting the ball off,
a whole game of just me running, running, running,
but never even getting over the scrimmage line.

I can't cope with all these pressures, Lord.
They tell me I should include recreation, reading, prayer,
family time, church time, work time,
plus, Lord, I want to do, do, do. . . .
I look around at the undone,
and the deadlines ahead—
only a machine could spit all that out!

Lord Jesus, you lived here only 33 years,
and spent only three of those ministering.
You had the whole world's troubles
square on your back.
You were sent to change the entire world.
Just you—all by yourself.
Neat assignment!

But you did it.
Thirty years were enough.
Three years were enough.

I notice, Jesus, you never planned
without talking to your Father.
You spent so much time with him
you knew you were completing *his* plan.
You couldn't heal everyone,
nor convert everyone,
nor teach everyone,
nor gain every insight.
It didn't matter—
you concentrated on your Father's plan.

Lord, when I bring my hassles to you;
when I say, "Lord, here I am,
I'll stop everything,
start anything,
whatever you say,"
that's when I'm calm.
It's actually fun, Lord,
to be in the press of a thousand details
but totally relaxed inside,
knowing that one thing done is enough;
knowing I'm energized by you.

Lord, I'll be in rough and tumble all my life—
the world's needs keep building
and the pressures don't ease.
But if I look to you, Jesus,
as you did to your Father—
if I really believe in your plan—
I'll move in your peace and power.

※ THE OLD ONES ※

My fingers play a game, Lord,
in the softness of my lover's hair. . . .
It's like new kittens' fur,
but long, very long—
heaps of dandelion fluff blown to the wind;
a waterfall to impudently push my face into.
Young, saucy, come-get-me hair—
with the same liveliness as
her eyes, her mouth, her nose against mine. . . .

Imagine
my lover's hair gray-white, crackly, wispy—
a mere scrap of decency
on her aged skull with its dull eyes,
drooping mouth.

Being old. Isn't that a thousand centuries away?
No.
Each month goes faster;
we hurtle through the years.

I drive by them on the street—
escapees from that sagging frame building . . .

43

old men in wrinkled wash pants
walking vacantly toward the coin wash . . .
old women staring numbly at the traffic,
maneuvering as if they'd never walked when young.

I read yesterday about an old actor
who said he felt as if he were
a young man only last week,
but had suddenly been set upon,
mugged,
stuffed into his old skin.
Outrageous, this young man
suddenly trapped in parchment skin with brown spots,
peering out of it through watery, myopic eyes,
all mustered up for dying and pity.

We who are young
fear age more than death.
Fear the humiliation
of becoming a "messy problem"
who can't control bladder or brain.
I read of Africans who say
people look forward to getting old there—
it's an honor to have white hair.
Why not here?

I remember Jeanette's grandmom saying,
"I'm ready to die right now,"
and there was cheer in her voice
and a happy resolution—no fear, no regrets,
as she painfully served us lunch.
Two years later I looked at her tortured body,
a thin specter laid out among the flowers.

It didn't look at all like her,
and I wondered why she had to suffer so.

Yet, I must admit, Lord,
she showed your love all the way through.
And if I fear her fate worse than death,
I know you've said,
"Perfect love casts out fear."
It did for her. . . .

I wonder how enthused she must be now,
bustling about up there with you,
understanding, now, the pain down here.
I can just see her
making meals or humming or figuring out a new solution
in whatever work or pleasure you've dipped her into.
This I know—
she's not sitting on a cloud
grumbling about what happened here.

Years ago in my crib, Lord,
I looked up at parents, uncles, aunts.
Now I'm old enough to know
that probably I'll bury every one of them.
It's rather gruesome to think of,
that each one will shrivel, lose faculties,
that one by one they'll leave me.
But each will be released to you, and joy.
As I touch their wrinkled skins,
let me touch with love.
Let me feed toothless jaws,
listen to their mental wanderings. . . .

Lord, even as I say it,
I rebel!

I want to escape them, and my own fate.
But the seasons of life are set,
as surely as birth and pain and passions.
I cannot neatly shield myself
from the mundane dribblings of our bodies.
And love never means reaching out
just when I feel like it.

The good:
Laughter. Kisses. Tennis. Passion. Tasting.
The terrible:
Pain. Ice. Leukemia. Scalpels. Blindness.
None are as important as your presence!
The most tedious days are joy, Lord,
when you are alive inside me.
And you will be forever in me—
you promised that,
even when I'm old. . . .

�֎ THE SPECTACULAR YOU ✷

Dull.
Tedious.
Archaic.
I'm afraid, Lord,
you have a very bad image.
You thought up all sorts of bizarre creations:
red sea anemones and imperial angelfish,
sexual tinglings and shaking laughter,
volcanic spectaculars of orange-red smoke-birthing islands,
yet your followers have somehow gotten the idea out,
that you're terribly drab.

People drive by churches
and see weathered gray tombstones beside them,
and it's almost as if those gravestones spread—
like a field of marble mushrooms inside the church,
standing tilted and cracked in the pews,
and a tall, cold-gray one in the pulpit
with engraved words dated 1881.
How does the image get there, Lord,
into people's brains when church and God flit by?

We sing hymns a hundred years old,
and march in to ritual. . . .
Lord, we need the truth of history,
and ritual is a necessary root.
But we can't live in yesterday's songs.
We can't wrap you up in them.
You are *today!*
How could we think you're outdated—
you who hold the universe together?

Are churches really tombstone warehouses?
The world thinks so.
A TV quiz show has more snap
than the gray image of ancient Jesus holding lambs:
This man who let soldiers nail him to a cross
(*no swashbuckler, this Jesus*),
just a quiet country boy made good,
but caught in his religionizing,
and executed, poor fellow.
But he said nice things,
and his followers got his ideas into a book,
but it's boring stuff,
no plot, just no-no's,
like don't booze and play around.

Lord, not even *Superstar* or *Godspell* cracks your image:
They dress you in clown clothes to brighten you up—
John Wayne they put in greasy buckskin;
but to you they add greasepaint and spangles.

Jesus, you held the entire universe under your fingernail,
then spun it off billions of years ago,
to become solar system, Milky Way,

out to the quasars and pulsars—
and who knows what they'll find.
This man they whipped and killed
was the Creator of the universe, God himself.

Words, words, words,
we're so saturated with theology sounds:
Jesus Christ, Son of God, Second Person of the Trinity.
Do we know what that means?
The awesome claim?
When you said you could have called
legions of angels to protect you—
well, *at least!*
You made the noon and tides,
the heat of all suns,
the tons-per-inch weight of white-dwarf stars,
paramecium and mockingbirds,
frost fantasies and gnus.
Scientists say that,
probing smaller than molecules, electrons,
something mysterious holds us together,
some glue, some force. . . .
Your Word says that by you,
"all things consist, cohere, are held together."
If you—Jesus—let go,
if you held your breath,
nothing.
Extinction.
Foolish to believe all that?
Perhaps.
But certainly not dull—
that you, who created energy and trees,
allowed human muscles and jeers to gibbet you.

You brought us life beyond biology.
Life as unique as that which separates
a leopard from a stone.
You transformed that repugnant electric chair;
that gruesome executioner's tool,
the cross,
into a symbol of triumph and joy,
to be worn around a girl's neck.
Who set you up, Lord,
as a bore?
You weren't to the Romans!
Certainly not to the spluttering Pharisees!
And not to anyone who sees you alive—
right now, in us.

HOT FUDGE MACHINES

Failure.
It's not easy to live with, Lord.

I know a girl who flunked school,
had a baby at fifteen.
She can't type,
she can't sort envelopes,
she can't even make milkshakes at the drive-in.
She gets fired every three days or so.
Like a ragamuffin from Appalachia,
a misfit here in the suburbs,
she's a walking failure, Lord.
How does she live in her skin?

Lots of "neat" people fail, too, Lord.
I sat with a friend who was bright and energetic,
full of ideas and competence and concern.
But he got fired, Lord,
in spite of all that,
and the wounds in his eyes haunted me.
He had to face his friends,
and himself.

Failure.
You're rolling along,
people respecting you,
and suddenly you're the one who blew it.
I fear that, Lord.
What would it do to me?

Past failures have been stepping stones, mostly.
In analytic geometry one day I got an F.
Number twenty-four out of twenty-four students.
Worst in the class!
I squeezed my eyes shut, then glared.
I worked like next week was the Olympics.
And I got an A,
number one out of twenty-four.

Lord, even as I write about that,
I feel pride;
I could always overcome failure,
if not in one thing, then another.
But what if deep failures smashed into me,
probed icily to the core of me?
Would my whole self-concept abort?
Would I, failure after failure after failure,
melt inside, like Dali's limp watches?

A friend sat down beside me one day
and said he'd learned something heavy.
He'd just failed—
and he was glad.
He'd worked at a project for months,
and it had blown apart.
Now he was saying,
"If I hadn't failed,

I'd never have learned about myself.
Or what God was trying to say to me."

That's what you've done to me, Lord.
Given me little failures that teach.
But deep failure—
would it make me a whiny baby,
lashing out, blaming others?
Or would I grow at my core
because you are there?

Actually, to fail in abilities isn't serious.
But to fail morally—
to fail you, Lord,
is bitter and tragic.
Why is it, Lord,
that I'm more afraid of failing before people
than to fail in front of you?

I drove an ice-cream truck one year,
spilled the hot fudge machine *all* over everything
and nicked a tree with a fender.
Got fired.
And I don't want to admit that,
cause friends will think,
Hey! He's the clod I thought he was after all.
But you, Lord,
you watch my failures every day
and I don't care what you think—
as I reach for pie gluttonously;
as I stare raptly at a sexy come-on;
as I say nothing while others put down a neighbor.
You see me every second, Lord,
yet I care more what humans think.

Lord, you love me as I am.
A failure. A success. Either way.
I am somebody because you love me.
That's all! No other reason.
You love me.
You call me to success,
to high aspirations.
But it's like watching a thunderstorm
roaring, pelting, splashing, blackening, streaking.
It's a great show,
but I'm not the storm.
And neither am I accomplishments and poise.

Thanks for loving me, Lord—
thunderstorm or drizzle.
Just don't let me be a stagnant pool.
Splash all over me, Lord,
throw anything at me!
Make my drive to success center in
yielding to you,
enjoying you,
and loving you . . .
the way you love me.

✖ HOBIE CAT ✖

Wow! What am I riding?
The wind is gentle,
but this Hobie Cat rips through waves like a speed boat.
How do sail and jib,
with the wind against us,
whip us so spanking fast across the lake?

All my life I've felt the wind—
on my face,
ruffling my jacket,
cooling my feet.
But I never let it take me anywhere.
What a ride!

Lord, sometimes—
when I think of children taught to hate,
and people exploiting in your name,
and the brutality of your planet—
I feel "You don't care. How could you?"
But the wind of your Spirit touches me,
gives me life.
How can I deny that?

When I hoist my sails,
You fill them,
and whoosh my catamaran through the waves.

People picnic on the shore.
I see them over there, Lord.
Have they felt the wind in their sails?
I sense your presence.
How can I reject you,
just because people on the shore insist
wind rustles leaves, and nothing more.

Out here in the Hobie Cat, Lord,
zinging along with sail flapping,
I can't explain how the wind works.
But it does.
And I know you fill me
with motion and joy.
Take me somewhere, Lord.
Your somewhere.

❊ STRANGERS ON A BUS ❊

This talking to you, Lord.
Does it mean anything?
Do you answer?

I remember praying for weeks, Lord,
about that thirty-two-hour bus trip.
I pleaded with you,
demanded even,
that you make it very, very special.
I was going to a seminar
on how to win kids to you,
and I wanted you to be in me.

Wow—what a bus ride!

A blizzard swallowed us in Pittsburgh.
We changed buses
and my lunch ended up traveling East
while we windshield-wipered toward Kansas City.
Everybody hungry.
Everybody riding all night,
hours behind schedule.

A camaraderie built.
We sang and told stories.
Up and down the bus
we stumbled and laughed
and we grimaced at the thick, white flakes.

My three closest seat mates
traveled with fresh pain.
An air force sergeant, about twenty-one,
just back from Korea,
returned to his young wife,
and found her gone.
She and his little son
now lived with another man.

An eighteen-year-old girl with strawberry-red hair—
like a Breck girl on the back of *Seventeen*—
rode with her month-old baby.
Hours before, she'd left her husband . . .
and now she was riding "home."

A Mexican woman, about twenty-five,
dark and handsome as a flamenco dancer,
had been thrown out by her rich husband.
"Only six months married," she told me.
"I was number four, and now he's done with me.
I was just another toy."

The three of them rode together,
sharing their grief with each other,
with me in the middle of them.

Coincidence?
That I had prayed so hard
and found myself among broken people?

I sat with the sergeant and listened,
and empathized
and tried to show him your hope.

In the middle of the night
the Mexican woman and I conversed softly,
and tears edged my eyes as I listened.
The bus ground through gray slush and stopped.
I looked at the red light
and the store signs barely lighting her face.

"Want to pray?" I asked.
"Yes. Yes, please. But how?"

I talked to you, Lord,
then she did.
She asked you into her life that night, Lord,
as we talked and talked about you.

We drove off the highway
to an old grocery store.
We jumped through snow drifts to it.
Our bus load emptied the shelves
and picnicked, walking through snow
and boarded again festively satisfied,
singing Christmas songs though it was January.

We stopped in a one-street town in Missouri.
A mom and dad waited
and the red-haired girl stepped out with her baby.
They moved awkwardly to hug her,
their daughter, tight-lipped, suffering.
As the Greyhound noised away
I watched the snowy wind attack the baby blankets

59

and the old father grabbing suitcases,
the three figures gray and alone in the white swirls.

Pulling away from that young mother
and looking at the stone-faced sergeant
and the dark beauty with timorous new hope,
my emotions fused into a bittersweet ache.
I sensed the joy of linkage with you,
and needing to reach out to people.

Somewhere near the Missouri line,
we stopped at a station.
I carried the woman's suitcases as she changed buses.
I wanted to hold her tight like a sister,
and even cry a little,
but we just shook hands,
and we stared at each other through the window
as the Greyhound weaved around the stanchions.

✠ A LOUSY, WONDERFUL DAY ✠

Lord, you shamed me into it.
I've been so listless the last months,
not believing anything mattered,
my fingers, eyes and brain dull as sand-rubbed glass.

So I got up at six,
walked in the fog,
sat at water's edge by cattails,
mists making it a fantasy world,
and asked you for one thing:
a good day.

Trite, huh?
Just one day when I'd feel your Presence.
One day you'd give me energy, joy,
the desire to live,
to participate.

And the strangest thing happened.
All through the frustrations and stupidities,
yesterday for the first time in months,
it was a great day!

Lousy mistakes and boredoms, yes,
but inside me,
a great day.

And this morning, I spent forty minutes
praying for some people,
and asking for the same thing.
And you did it again!
Today was grubby work,
watery diet pop,
tiresome phone calls,
but a great day!
You were with me!

If you don't exist,
like so many say,
how come I felt integrated,
full of purpose,
the only difference between these two days
and ninety preceding,
was saying, "One thing I want, Lord—
you!"

When you're with me—
What a great day!
Can we make it three for three, Lord?
I'll meet you in the morning.

BEAT 'EM!

Competition. Smash. Jab. Lunge.

Is it wrong, Lord,
this trying to beat out opponents?
To ram my shoulder into a guy?
to body-check him–hard?
to slap away his best shot?
All of life is competition.
Is it wrong, Lord?

When we were kids,
I tackled my brother in a back-yard game.
Years smaller than he,
I grabbed his ankle
and rode him thirty yards before
I tripped him–
Thunk! . . . into the hard November ground.
He looked across at me,
surprised.
"Way to go, kid," he grunted–
and the rest of that day,
I was a tiger!

Couldn't competition be like that sometimes,
Lord?
Admiring the brother who outdoes you . . .
but still fighting like crazy to win?

The Bible doesn't say much about sports . . .
that was for the Greeks those days—
running naked, shocking the Jews.
But Paul must have known about the Olympics,
cause he said to run the race—
run it to win!

Lord, I know how Paul wanted me to compete:
to fight my laziness,
my selfishness,
my desire to quit,
my tendency to shove you into a corner,
and run my life my way.

Competition grinds away laziness,
polishes and lifts—
lifts me to heights I didn't think possible.
Competition demands my best,
and that is of you.
Must I envy someone who writes best sellers
or makes an A
or hits a home run?
Or can I rejoice in
his art,
his intelligence,
his power?
I am your child, Lord,
unique,

loved.
I don't have to be what others are!

Opponents are made in your image, too.
I'm glad for the people you've made,
for the way they stretch out
when they run like deer;
for the jumps they make
that leave me standing;
for their toughness.
I drive to excel—
I'll block their shots,
grab them and drag them down.
That's the twist, the paradox,
the life you put me in, Lord.

I know it is evil,
to want to pulverize an opponent,
to go after him like an enemy to be destroyed,
when I look at him,
not as your creation,
but as a thing to be humiliated.
When I jab and gouge . . .
not just with my fingers, but with my spirit.

Sometimes I wish life weren't like it is—
always competing against nature,
germs,
death.

Yet your book tells me,
"We are more than conquerors
through Him who loved us."
Your power, Lord,

is that of a billion suns.
You live within me,
telling me to love,
even as I compete.
Strange paradox.
But you did it on the cross.
You defeated Satan, and gave us victory.

※ COURAGE IN THE VALLEY ※

Lord, thank you
for creating Christians like Dave and Elsbeth.

We had dinner with them last night.
Her Swiss smile at first looks almost shy
as she peeks out of her young, crinkly eyes.
She's warm, open, full of love and life,
and her shyness gets washed away by all that.

We had visited Longwood Gardens,
hardly able to absorb the thousands of
orchids, cacti, banana trees and palms. . . .
We had laughed and told stories,
and she told of hibiscus in her home in Nigeria
where she worked as a nurse "in the bush."

Dave talked of their wedding day four years ago.
They had spent the early morning hours together
above Berne, Switzerland,
staring at the Alps.
Near them were gravestones and they thought,
Most of these people had wedding days, too.

67

Did they think then of ending up here?
"We resolved to think of our graves,"
Dave told me as we walked past a Japanese cherry tree.
"We decided to live with eternal values.
But we didn't realize it would be so soon."

Elsbeth is full of humor;
she looks, laughs, tells stories.
How can she have acute leukemia?
Right now, as she walks with us,
she's fine—she's in remission.
But she'll be fortunate to live a month or two.

She loves you, Jesus,
and it shows in her attitudes.
But the terrors of treatments and death
run through her brain and emotions.
She's too young to die!
Does that sound like a cliché?
How can it be?
She'll leave two baby boys.
She'll leave her lover—so soon! So soon!

Elsbeth had a dream last night.
She was on a boat
and black persons were clinging to the sides.
A white man kept stamping on their hands,
forcing them into the water to their deaths.
Elsbeth went to others on the boat,
pointing the man out, saying,
"Look what he's doing.
He's already killed people."
Someone confided to her,
"He's after you because you're telling on him."

Elsbeth saw him at a window, then,
aiming a gun at her.
She was terrified.
She called for the police, who arrested him—
but then—inanely—they let him go!
She felt the same terror—
he was at the window again,
aiming at her again.
Elsbeth awoke so shaken,
she literally couldn't move.

I remember, Lord,
long before the diagnosis
the unique magic in Dave and Elsbeth's love.
Their courtship story of Land-Rovers,
the young, single doctor getting rebuffed,
her driving him out to a bush clinic—
it's a three-hour treat of fun and deep laughter,
and seeing your hand, Lord, in putting them together.
They're delightfully in love, Lord.
So *she's* the one to get leukemia!

Lord, it almost crushes them,
this terrible weight.
Yet they stand.
To see their faith in you
and Dave's tough questions about what you're doing—
it makes you real, Lord.
I can see you alive in them.
They have so much to lose,
yet they believe.
They believe you love them,
that you weep with them—
that you hate this disease with them.

Their faith isn't phony, Lord.
It could so easily be a thin shell,
to hide from death's reality.
But they face Monster Death head-on.

Lord, thank you for Dave and Elsbeth.
They make alive your psalms of trusting,
even when the enemy's spear impales;
even when walking toward death
and leaving everything you love. . . .

Thank you, Lord.

※ OTHER DIMENSIONS ※

Yes, Lord, I'm glad I'll die someday.
Heaven won't be sitting on clouds,
playing harps and bored with "goodness."
Jesus, you said, "I and my father work."
What will you have me doing?
Exploring planets and starting new cities?
Building a house?
Communicating to cultures beyond earth?
Entering dimensions of your bizarre creatures
who work and play and delight in you?

On earth, families break up, hatreds grow—
I can do so little to change things.
But in other worlds,
when you're fully in charge
and the evil one's been sacked—
now that'll be different!
Lord, my mind goes wild
thinking of you in charge—really in charge.
Praise you, Lord.
I see what the Apostle Paul meant
when he said that to die was better.

I'll stay here till you call me.
Just let my brain spin with thoughts
of what your next worlds will be like . . .
and help me bring a taste of that to planet earth.

❊ PLAYMATE MOTHERS? ❊

Lord, I have to admit
that all these magazines and books
that sell sex like it's deodorant
lure my eyes as I walk by.
They taunt my sex hungers,
always coming with naked skin
and moist mouths.

But they also make me angry, Lord.
With the fervor of a new religion,
they preach sex as a cure-all,
unwrapping mysteries and subtle delights:
"Shed your hang-ups with your clothes!"
One science fiction novel depicted
a whole planetful of people wonderfully happy—
no wars, no bickering, everyone gentle and courageous
because anybody could make it with anybody—
father/daughter, sister/brother, mother/son.
With repressions gone, all was peace and love.
What imbecility!

"Sex is normal,
nude is natural.

If it feels good, do it!"
So the profit makers package it—
full-color pages with skin impeccably highlighted.
It sells; it's part of free enterprise,
people want it,
so it must be ok,
and it sure beats puritanism!
So they sell, sell, sell
the good life and the refined sexual appetite
(which includes anything at all, of course).
Sell the delicately highlighted, antiseptic girls
who obviously do not menstruate
or have the wrinkled bellies of motherhood,
for babies being birthed with screams and blood
between a playmate's bronze-tanned legs—
Unthinkable!
For nude is natural,
sex is recreation—
a simple function to enjoy.
So they sell the slick voyeurism
for a buck or two a copy
(beats standing on milk boxes looking in windows).
No neuroses.
No guilt.

Let's jump in the pool—
all together now,
Let's do something new and naked;
toss in an animal—why not?
the jokes need some "daring" sex.
And consumers not only buy,
and turn on,
with this "socially redemptive" porn,
but believe.

For it comes in finest quality,
and is packaged with terribly deep thinking,
sanctified by musing pipe smoke.

How'd we get here, Lord?
How'd we make our view of sex so shallow
and lose the beauty of it?

Let's face it, Lord,
religionists gave playboys the vacuum!
It was supposedly Christian to blush at sex,
to disdain ecstacy.
They allegorized Solomon's sexy Song.
With these forces rumbling through our bodies,
no wonder people laughed when preachers said,
"Your organs are there only for procreation.
If you enjoy it,
it's lust; it's sin."
Where'd they get those ideas—
husbands and wives afraid to touch?
Did they read their Bibles
with Saran Wrap over their brains?
Lord, why do you allow people
to misrepresent you like that?

Now we're drenched in the other extreme,
and all this pubic peering and leering
hasn't exactly liberated us to joy.
Are days so drab,
life so blah,
that people search their beds
and playmates' bodies
out of utter boredom?
Nothing better to do.

Maybe sex would be exciting.
One gets the picture
of a Thanksgiving dinner two hours after—
people still nibble on a turkey breast,
wishing it tasted as good as the first hungry bite.

So they must go further,
with a compulsion for more, more, more,
just one more variation.

Sex—
with no encounter of persons:
Just like a handshake, that's all.
Like taking a drink.
Any sex is normal.
So they play around with the organs
and lose the mystery of two God-children becoming one.
Evading long-term responsibility,
they refuse to be long-term lovers.
So where, then, are the long-term fathers?
They make complex forces simple
and market the lie.
Sack out with anyone handy.
Of course you need a mature relationship,
and you shouldn't use people.
What happens when one gets bored
and the other doesn't?
FIRED PLAYBOY BUNNIES FIGHT BACK
said a headline last week.
Seems they were getting a bit old,
like sex partners do.

"Be content with the wife of thy youth;
let her breasts satisfy thee at all times. . . ."

76

Your book, Lord, is not only frank,
it puts persons before passion.
For you made sex,
and you care about joy and pleasure both.
Sex is for those who love,
who have a commitment!
Nothing less.
It's more than an ecstatic handshake.
Two persons become one!

Saying sex is recreation—nothing more—
is like saying breakfast
is nothing more than tickling taste buds.

Lord, the language of the body,
of sexual communication,
is powerful and beautiful.
Help me never to lie
with my lips against lips.
Help me not to say with my body,
I love you,
when I do not love at all.

※ ROUGH LUMBER ※

This park in the center of town, Lord—
what an oasis!
White, graveled paths,
flowering trees,
center fountain,
and blossoms thick, planted in perfect symmetry.
Nowhere in the woods would I find
a park like this:
waves of rich-organdy petals,
edged by burnt orange and greens,
with red berries thick on bushes;
and a precisely planned aurora bourealis of blossoms
everywhere.

Thanks, Lord, for letting man be your partner.
It's as if you tossed us rough lumber
and said, "Build. Shape. Create."

Man and God.
A team!
Lord, here are my hands.

Let me plant. Prune. Shape. Touch.
Create beauty,
with you.

✖ SOMEONE IS ALWAYS STARVING ✖

Lord, how do I live
with her photo burning out of the magazine
lying neatly on my walnut end table?
She looks fourteen,
a beautiful oriental girl,
gentle-faced in a war-ripped village,
a bony babe in her arms.
"The baby will die any hour,"
the caption reads: "Her breasts have no milk."
Fourteen. She looks like someone I know—
an exchange student?
I want to reach into the photo,
give her food,
a touch of fingertips to cheek,
some hope.

I wonder who snapped the picture.
White? Well fed? Robust?
How could he photograph her
and write those captions
instead of feeding her?

But he had tens of thousands to feed
or photograph.
He's there to report; to awaken the world;
to jolt someone.
Me?
Or will I simply write about her?

She stares numbly, her face innocent—
too innocent for the death-knowledge soaked into it.

Her picture lies there in the magazine,
black hair against bronze skin,
blackmailing my joy.
What should I do about it?
I could frame it,
lovely colors,
on charcoal matting and aluminum frame.
It could remind me of the suffering.
Ignore it?
Toss the magazine like other throwaways?
Someone is *always* starving.
An earthquake,
a war,
a drought,
a flood.
Every day a new catastrophe.

Sometimes I wish TV would go bankrupt;
that magazines, newscasts and jets would quit shrinking
        our world.
It used to be simpler—
help your neighbor.
Someone starving on your block?
In your town?

Get out there and help!
Flooded out?
Dig out your denims and blankets!

No one drenched or homeless walks by me.
But they're around,
in shacks in Louisiana,
high rises in Hong Kong,
and a house around the corner.
They're in Africa, Indonesia, Bangladesh,
but that's another universe.

What should I do?
Send a check to World Vision,
for the cute orphans in the ads?
I'm young, healthy, rich.
Oh, most would say,
"No—you're just getting by."
But I'm rich compared to those
who dig broken fingernails into despair.
It's right, isn't it, for me to be stylish?
To watch *National Geographic* specials on color TV
(How could you watch birds and sunsets on black and
        white?).
It's right to drive a car that won't kill in traffic,
isn't it?
To use deodorant, shampoo, skin spray, toothpaste, foot
        powder, creme rinse, after shave?
To buy ties, shirts, jackets, shoes, socks
that aren't junk, that will last?
To plan trips and recreation and enriching experiences?

Yes! God delights in all good things.

But is it *priority* in a raw jungle?
The tie I just bought would feed a family in Haiti for a
    week.
The used car I bought would feed twenty Indonesians for
    a year.

It's too complex!
Who's the fool with an easy answer?
Western economy produces for people,
and God is a God of beauty and bounty,
even extravagance,
to judge by his variegated planet earth,
his vast, inexplicable universe.
God doesn't want artists to starve,
or to end up digging utilitarian ditches.
He made the artist to paint,
as he made the lion to roar.

But our world's twisted—
a billion selfish acts a day blind us.

Perhaps we are called to die for one another,
in a thousand different ways.
It chills me, Lord, reading the Old Testament.
It keeps hammering at our obligations to the poor,
right in the same breath as wrath and judgment.
And Jesus!
Your whole life was giving,
               giving,
               giving.

No easy answers.
I don't expect one,
for you, God, are a Person,

not a code or set of principles.
You yourself are the answer,
for you confront us,
love us,
nudge us minute by minute
as we yield everything we are—
dollar bills and car payments,
and our rights to ourselves.
You won't let us off the hook.
Those faces of starving kids
will keep coming into my living room,
shoving me up against you—
forcing me to say, "What, Lord?
What's my part?"

I can't ignore them.
And I can't reach out frantically,
trying to feed the world,
pacify the world,
cleanse the world,
and go utterly mad.
I have to confront you, to find my role.

Lord, stop me from being so complacent.
I'll say all this to you,
then forget before lunch.
I'll do it again and again
because my little microcosm is all I care about.
Do I really love some oriental kid?
I turn the page, switch channels,
or take the dog out.

Lord, let that child-mother's face
hang in front of me like a movie screen,

her face and the paraplegics',
and the psychologically amputated,
the schizophrenics,
the spiritually bankrupt.
You once said, Jesus,
"This is the measure of your greatness:
your service to others."
You've said that's the path to joy.

Show me, Lord.
Show me what I should do—*today*.

※ ANGRY, LOVING GOD ※

Great News!
A marvelous bulletin about you, Lord!
You don't hate us.
You're not an ogre.
You're no impetuous rock thrower
or lustful, capricious Greek god.
Good news!
Your book says you love us,
you died for us.

Romans and Greeks and Norsemen saw you
as moody, sullen, irascible—heroic but flawed.
Now, of course, we're scientific—
we denude you of emotions
and call you "The First Cause Uncaused,"
and "Ground of Being."

But you're a Person.
You feel anger and pain,
delight and pleasure,
all in the beauty of holiness.
Lord, you are love.

You care about me.
You are not half evil, half good.

That's a marvelous discovery!
That's the best news possible on this wracked planet.
You really are love,
the Father of lights,
the source of all joys.

Praise you, Lord,
just for being you,
and for having victory over the evil one
who will one day be zapped for all time.

Good news! You're in ultimate charge.
You're the God of love.
Hallelujah!
I'm glad you're you, Lord,
and that you've shown in Jesus
what you're really like.

※ PLUNGE ※

The air is a hot, muggy blanket.
I stand at a lake edge,
toes digging at gravel.
The chill around my toenails is sharp.
A whole foot?
The water shocks it as I shove it in.
Both legs?
My sticky body shudders
as the ice water jabs above my knees.
Auuuuugh! Now my suit is wet.
My belly cramps as I plunge my shoulders under.
Brrrrrrrrrr!

Three minutes later,
I look at the mountains around the lake,
swim out to the raft. . . .
I'm no longer sticky,
nor muggy,
I'm utterly refreshed,
splashing around like a just-released puppy.

Lord, I'm like that with you, aren't I?
I stand all sticky and miserable

in a world without refreshment,
and I know that splashing into contact with you
could energize and delight.
But I don't want your control.

Yet I know—
I absolutely know—
that when I'm immersed in you,
life becomes a splash
into your dynamics.

Help me to plunge in, Lord.

✳ THE RED-HAIRED WAITRESS ✳

Her red hair is piled neatly on her head
in one of those graceful Grecian styles,
and even in pouring my coffee
she tilts her head in self-assurance,
smiling with that warmth
of someone who knows she's pretty and liked.

What's she heading for,
she and these other cute girls
balancing plates and scribbling orders.
"I'm the only virgin in this place,"
one of them said to me.
They go to bed,
have their little adventures—
they seek love, the permanent stuff,
but it crumbles as it hits the nitty gritty.
They have magic dreams
of curling up with a guy
who will share and bring a fun-filled life.
But most find short-term sex
and short-term marriages.

91

"How's everything in your life?"
I ask her blandly.
"Oh, I don't know."

Will this red-haired, saucy innocent find
the delights of touching both body and soul?

Lord, I pray for these girls,
and the guys they'll love.
Lord, get into their lives.
Fulfill their dreams.
Show them *your* joys—
of two persons joining hands with you
to serve you
and therefore each other.

Explode into their lives, Lord,
and mix their dreams with reality.

✖ EGGS ON THE FREEWAY ✖

I walked past some kids today, Lord—
ten-year-olds making the sidewalks alive
with swirling flag patches,
flashing street-hockey sticks,
yells and pleadings and intrigue.
And right in the middle of them
a boy sat in a wheel chair,
trying to join in,
to yell at the right times,
to be more than a tree stump or a bush.

It's maddening, Lord.
That boy is meant to run and shout and chase.
His nerves and glands and muscles are a marvel—
an incredible creation of yours—
but he's like a drenched butterfly.

One damaged gland incapacitates.
One pull on a wheel kills.
What a dangerous world we're in!
Pascal said it:

"A drop of water or a draft of air
can kill a man!"
How can you make us so complex and marvelous,
then dump us here?
Lord, it's as if I held a living egg—
an embryo chick about to hatch—
and placed it on the freeway.
You birth our soft flesh in a world
where concrete and steel rip and shred.

Lord, I could look at the wheel-chair kid
and get all *Reader's Digesty* about him.
I could look for the kids who show compassion—
who make him fit in.
I could find the good adversity brings.
I could look for your ultimate purpose
(didn't you say you counted each hair on our heads?).
And, Lord, I'll happily admit it—
pain does build maturity in *my* life.
But the kid in the wheel chair?
Does he know you?

Lord, you talk to me of meaning,
of supernatural joys—
but most people belly through life in fear
never seeing past their fingernails.
Or, if they do see,
they know it's a squirrel-run without you.
There's nothing,
just crates and crates of eggs
spilled and rolling along the freeway
some cracked, some splattered,
some whole and happily rolling—
till the wheels hit them, too.

94

A lady at our church
takes care of foster kids.
Some arrive battered. Morose. Distrustful.
She gets them for a month or two—
and just as they start to open up,
to hug her and seek love,
the courts send them back
to parents who may beat them again
or bludgeon them with heavy words.
She watches a two-year-old boy play with his trucks.
Staying with her, he'd grow up loving.
With his parents, he'll live with hate,
and return hate,
and probably end up in prison,
or at least bitter and destructive.
She pictures that little boy,
starting to be lovable,
toddling into a cell.

Yes—there still is the *Reader's Digest*.
I suppose one out of 600 foster kids
will become a doctor or something.
And maybe the kid in the wheel chair
is more fully alive than any of us.
I know he could be—with you.
Help me, Lord.
Help me believe.
All I see tonight are broken eggs.

❋ SMOKE RINGS ❋

The young football star stood before us
as we ate our lunches
and told of reaching out for honors.
He'd gotten plaques and write-ups and letters
but they were like smoke rings.
"Not only do they disappear," he said,
"but when you put your hands around them,
they're nothing more than stale air."

Stale air!
What else is left to us children of change,
computerized, sorted and boxed?
Lord, not only are there no frontiers—
so what if there were?
One more book on a shelf?
Explore some unknown archipelago?
So what?

Everything's debunked.
Lord, who gives a rip!
So I push to excel, earn awards,
do my unique thing.

I read about a guy who drove himself
to win a national championship—
then shot himself the next day.
I know the psych books say that's logical—
a terrible low after a tremendous up.
But that's just the point.
The ups—
they're just stale air when you get there.
And without ups to drive toward,
why live?
Man once had a spirit of discovery.
"A new world full of gold and Indians."
Wow! That must have blown their minds!
"You can talk over a wire!"
"Have you heard of pygmys?
And people with bones through their noses?"
Now, the mystery is gone,
the only frontiers scientific.
You can see anything in living color,
and these days the natives
have Dole pineapple cans through their ears.

What's to commit myself to?
If I don't do my thing,
someone else will fill the hole.
Should I go out to nature,
saw boards and make a home—
be natural and respond to environment?
For what?
Zest. Delight. Love. Enchantment.
The words are owned by TV commercials,
for words have been glossed
and sold forever to soap and orange juice,
lipsticks and ice cream.

I read *The Lord of the Rings* once.
The Hobbit—little Frodo—
confronting monsters,
stumbling into sword fights,
gasping up mountains and over deserts,
all with incredible significance—
finally dropping the rings into fire and fury,
and changing everything.

What can I ever change, Lord?
What mountain can I climb,
what spidery horror slay
and feel the warm blood on my fingers?
I lie on my soft carpet,
sipping a 7-Up,
as Frodo crosses the desert,
as the hobbits evade the horrors searching them out,
their little bodies trembling, fatigued.

Lord, my world's too soft and solved,
pre-packaged and stamped.
I'm a piece of sheet metal rolling into a machine,
to be bent and cut and spat out
as a rather ordinary commodity.
Life's a multigrained, multicolored capsule
to swallow, and swallow, and swallow, and swallow,
and Lord, I'm so sick of swallowing the same thing!
Is my life really a pre-punched schedule
to ram my flesh through?

Yet, in some ways I'm like Frodo.
All these wastelands he traveled through,
day after day after day—

what a lot of nitty gritty!
His adventures, all compressed into the exciting parts,
keep me flipping pages,
eager to be there.
But how much of Frodo's fatigue
is just like mine?
How many of his apprehensions
are like mine when I face people I fear?
Am I part of an adventure,
and I don't even see it:
monsters of despair about to devour,
but your sword available, if I'll grab it?
These evil temptations
that would maul and bloody my dreams—
are they the terrors that stalk me,
the monsters to crush?

Lord, you also put into my road
broken people who need to be snatched
from terrors more hideous than those after me.
And I find myself in emotional deserts
wanting to evade mountains of discipline
that loom cold, like Everest.
Lord, I prefer Frodo's adventures
of boiling heat and terrible battles.

Or would I?

Are they here, Lord,
my adventures?
Are they really here?
Or are they part of a silly myth?
Am I living a flat joke, without a punch line?

Lord, to be part of the adventure,
I must *choose* the adventure.
To choose you,
a decisive, clear facing in your direction—
choosing between life,
or sleeping in my comfy hobbit hole;
choose between dull gasps
or throwing in my lot with Gandalf—
with you!
For when I choose,
you act.

Am I a bunnylike hobbit with a sword?
A laughable little human jousting evil gods?
No! Not I!
It's you in me.
And you whisper
"Call unto me, and I will answer,
and show thee great and mighty things. . . ."

You are life itself.
When I choose you,
enthusiasm grabs brain and emotions
—not constant, but deep-down steady in the will—
and you start feeding me ideas and reasons,
and the joy and dynamic to slay dragons of self-pity and
     lust.
To reach out to that kid
who needs to hear of your adventures
instead of vegetating in front of "Mannix."
Lord, there are so many of life's prisoners to free,
who never seek other options in life,
but muddle through, chained to conformity.
You are wrapped up in all sorts of adventures,

creating, painting, growing, warming, birthing.
And what a dramatist you are,
sending your son into this world.
You, who spun off worlds and suns,
created whales and microbes—
You became a little baby,
and we didn't even recognize you
as you smashed evil.

You destroyed the dark powers by your boldness,
your risk of staying with evil men thirty-three years.

The joy of doing something for someone,
for you, Lord,
beats finding a whole worldful of Indians and gold.
Who needs a new island to explore
when we're part of your adventure?
You seldom "solve" my problems,
but you change *me* through them,
and therefore a chunk of the world.

The weird—utterly weird—thing is,
sometimes I'd rather be a punched-out toy.
I'd rather reject you
and live *my* way.

Help me, Lord.

It's frightening, this leap into who-knows-what.
I don't like your demands, the sacrifices.
I like my own choices.
I love my pleasures,
and I'm afraid you'll snatch them.
I don't like the idea of days in the desert,

102

of a sword in my belly—
nasty words from powerful people.

Lord, grab me.
Force your way in!
Don't let me live like a plastic toy.
If I choose my own adventure,
I become a silly clown in the desert,
not to finally shout victory like Frodo,
but to mummify in absurd posture,
six feet from your bubbling springs.

Lord, my plan would be
to solve all the world's problems,
all by myself,
and I'd destroy myself in the process.
Who asked me to be James Bond for the world?
It's your adventure I'm called to,
not mine.
And when I choose your adventure,
I find mine.

And stale smoke becomes flame,
and dullness crackles into light,
to see into other worlds.